For lots of snuggles
& cuddles . . . Enjoy !
xoxo.
D.

Just You And Me

Written by P. Taylor Copeland

Illustrated by suzi Bliss kyle

Child of my child
Precious and dear,
A joy to my world,
My devotion quite clear.

Second chances for me,
Extra stories for you,
Lots of love and wet kisses –
My own déjà vu.

Play dates and visits,
One-on-one fun;
Cobwebs don't matter,
Chores go undone.

Innocent spoiling,
A cookie or two,
My arms always open
For hugs tried and true.

I cherish each moment
This time's not to waste;
Left behind handprints
Now kept not erased.

Grammy time, Grammy time,
I relish my role –
You my sweet angel
Have captured my soul.

XOXO and lots of love,

Patty-cake, patty-cake,
Peek-a-boo too.
My knee is a horsy –
Yaaa – hooo!!!

I tickle your tummy...
Where is your nose?
"This little piggy"
Plays with your toes.

Giggles and stories,
Oodles to see,
Grammy time, Grammy time –
Just YOU and me.

Quack-quack says the duck,
MOO says the cow,
Here
comes
the kitty,
You say me-o-www.

We pretend to be animals,
Some live in a zoo –
Monkeys and lions
And elephants too.

Giggles and stories,
Oodles to see,
Grammy time, Grammy time –
Just YOU and me.

We walk in the garden,
Spot bugs on the ground,
We smell the sweet flowers
And twirl round and round.

We swing on the swing
And slide down the slide;

We put sand in the bucket
And sit **side by side.**

Giggles and stories,
Oodles to see,
Grammy time, Grammy time –
Just YOU and me.

We toss lots of balls
And blow bubbles that pop;
Rover sits near
Should anything
drop.

We snuggle and cuddle,
Read **big** books with art –
Your wee little hands
Hold
the
strings
to my heart.

For Oliver

Just You And Me

© 2002 Grammy Time™ Books/P. Taylor Copeland
P.O. Box 639 San Luis Obispo, CA 93406-0639
Message/Fax (805) 541-3515
www.grammytimebooks.com
www.ptaylorcopeland.com

Designed by Ashala Nicols Lawler

Printed in China

ISBN 0-9712675-0-2

Giggles and stories,
Oodles **to see,**
Grammy time, Grammy time –
Just YOU and me.